SECRETS

The Secret Never Told You

Linda West

MORNINGMAYAN
PUBLISHING

With great love and gratitude to,
White Eagle, King David, and Sebastian

Contents

Prelude

Hi. I'm Linda West. It's nice to meet you!

I'm going to tell you how I came up with the formula I use to manifest quickly. I have used this process with my clients in my home practice and with students at my lectures. I have countless stories of the manifestations that occur once you begin to use this simple formula. I hope that you too will leave me testimonials of the wonderful things you create after learning my 5 easy steps to manifest.

After millions of people were made aware of the law of attraction by hits like *The Secret,* I noticed a large demand for the '*how to*' part that was never mentioned in the popular work.

People understood and believed it worked. They just didn't have any idea how to do it. That's why I wrote this book, to help you understand *how* to use *The Secret.*

I'm not going to give you the typical steps you've heard before on how to manifest. This is insider knowledge that even the experts don't want to share.

Too bad. The cat is out of the bag. I love you and you deserve everything. It's an abundant universe with more than enough for all of our dreams to come true. So if you found this, you deserve it, and I can't wait for you to get everything you love.

Along my unique and amazing spiritual travels, I listened and learned and tried to keep an open mind. What I realized was that each time I had been successful in manifesting something I wanted, it had followed a pattern. Subsequently, if I broke it down, I could teach others how to do it too. I began to teach my students in my lectures and home practice, with great success, but I never made my 5-step process public until now.

I don't much believe in mistakes or coincidences. I believe in signs, manifestations, and love. If you are reading this, then you are ready to be more powerful than you are now. You are ready for change and greatness and happiness.

In my lingo, you have raised your frequency.
Congratulations!

CHAPTER 1

How I Formulated the 5 Steps to Manifest

I'm on a flight to Dubai and I'm so excited.

I'm excited because I wished for this and it's actually happening. Just a month ago, I wished to be able to manifest traveling the world, and now that wish has come true.

It's happening in the most magical way — one which I never saw coming, and which involves no money.

Let's face it. If I had the money, I'd have been traveling the world already, right? Duh! People, 'wishing for world travel' is right up there on the list after 'becoming rich' and 'falling in love.'

In any case, most people don't have the resources to pick up and travel the world and neither did I, but that didn't stop me from wanting it, and 'wanting' gets you a lot of things.

> In fact, really really wanting with all of your heart,
> is one of the biggest keys to getting what you want.
> 'Wanting' and 'wishing' are actually the same thing.

The flight to Dubai takes 15 hours but it's not so bad because I'm in first class. Yes, hello, extra bonus points for the first class manifestation. Because remember, I'm not paying for this flight. It's free. I'm also going to be staying in one of the best hotels in Dubai, overlooking the entire port.

I know I'm going to have a great time because I'm going to make sure I manifest a great time, just like I manifested getting here.

I decided that this was the best time to begin my book on 'how to manifest' — while I was in the midst of one of my greatest manifestations!

This would come off as gloating if I wasn't going to show you

exactly how I did it.

> I'm just an average schmo like you,
> so if I can do it, you can do it.

When most people go after a dream, they will use their *mind* to figure out what to do.

If they are really determined, they will get their body involved in an *action* to make that dream a reality.

However, very few people know how to use their *spirit* and hearts to manifest their dreams.

That's the part I'm going to show you!

Soon, you will see magical things showing up in your life in miraculous ways, and the only thing you will have changed is getting your spirit involved and pointed in the right direction.

I'm going to take you through some simple lessons on how to make your wishes come true in 5 easy steps.

I'm going to teach you the true secrets *The Secret* never told you...

I am so excited for you!

After this book, you will realize that you have been creating your whole life, for the good or the bad.

You just woke up in the driver's seat. Now, where shall we go? :)

Let me explain to you a bit of my background and how it is that I learned about frequency and how I became the unknowing carrier of the torch of this sacred knowledge.

When I was five years old, I had a near-death experience. When I came back, I still had a clear connection to the divine realm. I had a full understanding of the 'Law of

Frequencies' at an intuitive level. (We all do, but it gets slowly shut down as we grow into the matrix.)

About 15 years ago, I started dreaming about triangles and math and time. I didn't understand the dreams, nor did I have a passion for mathematics in any way.

To be honest, I hated math and everything to do with math. I was an English major, mostly to stay *away* from math.

That said, when the dreams wouldn't go away, I decided I had better start keeping track of them and writing things down.

In my effort to understand, I started reading books that I normally would have never read or had any interest in.

I read books on quantum physics, string theory, vibration, and the Mayan Calendar.

I ultimately began to formulate the understanding of the 'Universal Science of Frequencies,' which later would become my first book, *Ultimate Power, The Use of Frequency Attunement.*

Based on my work, I ended up winning a scholarship from famed cultural icon and scientist, Terrence McKenna.

I was asked to go into the rain forest, with top scientists from around the world, to do the research. It was a transformative experience, which led to my understanding 'The Universal Science of Vibration,' which was shown to me in the form of 'Frequency Attunement.'

After the book was published, I went on to lecture every month

on 'The New Science of Frequencies.'

With the information I received through my dreams, and the research I did in the rainforest, I was able to develop a way to actually show other people how to step-by-step *create a wish* that comes true.

When we are younger, we tend to manifest things naturally, because one of the most potent parts of the process is loving something and having passion for it. We have a lot of that as children and less of it as adults, unfortunately.

Cultivate those childlike moments. They unconsciously bring you wonderful things and reduce your stress too.

One of the things I really wanted as a child, was to own a restaurant. I was so consumed with it as a young girl that at just six years old, I decided to open up my own restaurant out of my basement in Buffalo, New York.

I made a sign and put it outside on the snow bank in front of our little house. I called it the "Blue Suede Shoes Cafe." I had daily customers, despite the blizzard-like conditions.

I look back now and I wonder, "What kind of strange people were coming to a six-year-old's restaurant in her basement?" But that's another story.

The real focus is that I was building up to a future manifestation with this creation.

Unfortunately, I had reluctant landlords (i.e., my parents didn't like my running a restaurant out of our basement with my Barbie Burger Grill and my Easy Bake Oven).

One little ?re and they shut down my business. Go figure.

Despite the fact that it was short-lived, I put that frequency out there and years later, that frequency brought me my *real-life* restaurant *today*.

After I channeled the book on frequencies and began to apply what I knew on how to manifest, I started manifesting all sorts of magical things in my life.

One of those things that I manifested was the restaurant that two of my girlfriends and I bought and ran for eight years.

I manifested the restaurant that I had always wanted as a child, using the same technique I'm going to teach you now.

I also did it with none of my own money down. Heck, I was a single mom at that time and barely had money for the electric bill, let alone to go investing in a restaurant.

Remember, if I can do it, *you* can do it.

I didn't know how it was going to come through and you won't know how it's going to come through, but it will come, in a beautiful, amazing way — that I can assure you.

CHAPTER 2

Money Money Money

Okay, you need money. Everybody has it on the list. I can tell you how to get all the things that money can buy and if you still want cold hard cash, we can do that too. First, you will have to put up with my philosophy on why you can't focus on money, and then I'll show you how despite all that — yes, you *can* materialize cash.

One of the most important things you are going to have to realize is that to manifest, you have to let go and let the divine universe bring things in for you.

Now let that concept in. Let it just sink in for a moment.

In this world, at this time, the dominant belief structure is that you can only get things if you have *money*, that the only way to get what you want is through an *exchange of money*.

You have to set that aside because it will hold you back.

Sometimes you need to manifest cash, but almost always you need to manifest something you can *get* with cash.

Then there's the false assumption built that cash is the quickest and most direct way to acquire things you desire. This is completely incorrect.

Plus, there are a lot of things you can't acquire with money, like a good parking spot, a good friend, or a good attitude.

That said.....

The two things people always ask to manifest *first* are money and love.

Let's start with the easy one: money.

Almost always, people tell me they want to manifest money.

People assume that somehow, money is going to make them happy, change their lives, and bring them everything that's been standing outside the doorway to their bliss.

Believe me, I've been manifesting for a long time, and working with people trying to manifest for a long time. Almost always, you manifest what you want, or what your goal is, but it rarely shows up as cash.

The reason I say this is to not to depress you that you can't get your needs met. You can and you will. I'm just saying that a wad of money is not usually how it appears, although that may be the only way you see it now.

I'm asking you to be open to it coming in a surprising way – a way you wouldn't expect without money.

I know it sounds impossible, but I've been doing it now, and you'll do it as well.

Wait. Did I hear you screaming, "But what I need to manifest *is* money!"?

Okay, I understand you think that. And I will counter with, "What do you need the money for?"

Now, you may respond, "I need money to pay my rent and I don't have a job."

This is a valid wish: security and a safe home.

This is how we deal with this. First and foremost, the universe rewards those who move toward their desires, on all levels: mind, body, *and* spirit.

That said, if you need your rent paid, I recommend doing all the physical actions suited to fulfilling this (i.e., sell things, get more work, etc.). But then you should also be using the magical manifestation '5-step method.'

With this process, we approach manifesting *not* money,

but the *rent paid*. In this case, I work with a person to focus on the *rent being paid*.

The *rent paid* could then appear in many magical ways, some of which could look like this: a friend loans you money, you receive a check by surprise, you get a side job, somebody buys a painting you did,…etc.

Just remember, as we move through these exercises toward getting you what you want, that things may appear in ways you hadn't considered.

Don't get stuck in having to know.

That's why they call it 'magic.'

It's probably not going to come in the way that you think.

Here's a simple story to help illustrate what I mean. A fisherman will sit by the river with just one pole, hoping that a ?sh will come by, so he can have dinner. How much of a chance is there in catching your dinner if you only have one pole in the game?

That pole is akin to *people fishing for money.*

People are usually fishing for money to solve all of the

problems in their lives. Maybe the fishing pole is symbolic of their job. Maybe they even throw a little extra glimmering bait on the pole, such as a lottery ticket, but they are still fishing for the same game.

When you use the manifestation steps I will teach you, you will then open up to all of God's miracles and possibilities to help you. When you give up going after the money to get what you want, and instead focus on the *love* of the thing you want, then you enact all of God's universe to help you.

The universal divine fishing net then comes through, picking up all the possibilities you could have never imagined. There is a much better chance of getting your needs met than there is just trying to catch something with one little pole!

Are you starting to see where I'm coming from? Have you been counting on that one pole called *money* to fulfill all of your hungers?

Let me leave you with this famous poem by Goethe...

"Until one is committed, there is hesitancy, the chance to draw back. Concerning all acts of initiative (and creation), there is

one elementary truth, that ignorance of

which, kills countless ideas and splendid plans: that the moment one definitely commits oneself, then Providence moves too. All sorts of things occur to help one that would never otherwise have occurred. A whole stream of events issues from the decision, raising in one's favor all manner of unforeseen incidents and meetings and material assistance, which no man could have dreamed would have come his way. Whatever you can do, or dream you can do, begin it. Boldness has genius, power, and magic in it. Begin it now."

You still want cash. Understandable.

Thus, I'm going to give you my favorite tip for getting more cold hard cash.

Top tip: Love money.

Seriously, love your money as you spend it. Talk to it. Treat those little paper presidents like friends going out to bring you back more of their money friends. You always need more friends, right? :)

So often, we are afraid of our money or mad at it as we spend it. Money, like everything, is energy, so love your money!

Expect your money to leave your hands and bring you back more. Believe that more money wants to hang out with you. Learn to like money instead of fearing it. Talk to it, fall in love with it, and watch that cash bring home more of its friends.

Play with your money. See it as friend, not foe, and tell it to go and bring back more of the same. Get those little buddies working for you and tell them to stick to more cash and bring it back.

The point is we are afraid of money because most of the time we don't have enough of it.

Change your relationship with money. Love what you have, and when you spend it, pretend it's going out to seek more money for you, because things are magnetized to things that love them.

Love brings everything you love towards you so love money.

Now, do you see why the greedy 'money lovers' have so much? Unfortunately, many of those lost souls only love money. But you aren't a lost soul. You have room to love your wife, your kids, your cat — and some cash too, right?

Love it, but not above all else.

Money can't buy the number one thing
everyone wants....

and that is love.

Well done. Let's move forward.

CHAPTER 3

Love Love Love

The one thing that all my clients wish for is *love*. Now, love is a complicated thing. Ha ha. That's the understatement of the year!

When it comes to manifesting love, we very often have our sights set on a particular person.

Preferably, we should be focusing on the *feeling* we want to have with a partner, and then magnetize that *feeling* in a person, *to us*.

Love is a universal force on its own and goes hand-in-hand with divine timing. Thus, 'true love' is truly out of our human control.

Some people ask me, "Can I manifest love?"

I say "Yes, you can."

When they say, "But can I manifest love with the person

I want to love me?"

I say, "Sometimes."

But when they say, "Can I manifest true love?"

I say, "I don't know. I haven't done it yet. :) Only kidding. Ha ha."

As far as true love goes, that's in God's hands.

Here's an example from one of my clients and her experience using the 5-step process in her love life:

In my private practice, I was working with a girl named

Natalie. Natalie was devastated because she was having trouble in her love life. It was 6 AM and she was at my table, crying over her coffee.

I knew this was going to be a tough case because she was already in such a low frequency; it was going to be difficult to manifest anything positive.

She had recently gotten back together with an ex boyfriend. They had been apart for six years and he had recently initiated contact, and it looked like things were moving forward again.

They were going out on regular dates and talking to each other every day.

Then suddenly, everything just seemed to stall. He no longer seemed interested in pursuing the relationship and rarely initiated any calls.

Natalie was confused and sad.

It was the holidays and now he was barely returning her texts and emails. She was desperate and didn't know what to do.

The very first thing I did was attend to Natalie's frequency level.

I explained to her that she was going to need to stop crying if she wanted to get any good manifestation going. She couldn't do it from the level she was at.

Somehow, she would have to find a way to rally herself and pull herself up to a higher frequency.

I explained to her that we needed to either 'dead and bury' this relationship, in which case I would mourn with her, or she had better get herself into a 'faith' place that would allow a better outcome.

I started working with her in a movie form saying,

"Let's just imagine him showing up at your house. He's been really busy. He has some great reason; how would *that* look? What would that *sound* like?

When you feel it as real, then hold onto that feeling."

Needless to say, coaching her up to a higher frequency of belief, even imaginary belief, was difficult at this point because she was so down. We did our best to work through the process and she left in high spirits and was hopeful.

All throughout the day, she continued to call me crying, and I would continue to get her laughing, and then instruct her to imagine a good scene.

I told her to imagine something she wanted to occur right now, even something surprising, like him suddenly showing up at her door or accidentally running into him.

Maybe something would remind him of her and he would be

prompted to call her and ask her on a date.

Consequently, in the few minutes I worked with her, I could get her into a good frequency and thus, a believing place. Once she was in this better vibration, she would start to feel good again and I would say, "Okay, hold that."

Unfortunately, right after I would get off the phone with her, she would call an hour later, in the same state of hopelessness and disbelief.

As darkness fell, a worn out and defeated Natalie asked if she could call me one last time before she went to bed, because that was her most difficult time. I understood.

At about 11 o'clock that night, she called me. I picked up the phone, expecting to have to console her once again, and instead, she sounded completely different. In fact, she was bubbling with excitement.

I said, "What's up?"

She said, "He's here."

I said, "What?"

She said, "We are coming over!"

Ten minutes later, Natalie and her lover were sitting at the same breakfast table she'd just been at that morning, crying over her coffee (and waking me up at 6 AM).

Now, here he was, sitting with her at my table.

Natalie's explanation to me, later, went like this:

"Wow, what a coincidence! Seems he just happened to be in the neighborhood and thought of me and decided to just pop by at 11 o'clock at night and see if I was home..."

Hmm well, yes, what a coincidence that she got exactly what she had been manifesting since that morning!

Remember, I told you that when your wish comes through, very often you would be surprised? It's always a great surprise because it's a *gift!*

Needless to say, Natalie was elated, he was smiling, and I was happy for both of them.

Natalie had finally gotten what she wanted.

Or so it seemed.

Yes, Natalie had gotten what she wanted in the moment.

I knew that for certain, because he was sitting right in front of me.

However, I also knew that *love* has an agenda that works outside all the universal laws, because it *is* a law unto itself.

This wonderful reunion might have been the chance they needed to rekindle their romance, or it might have just been all the great white spirit could bring them, *because this love wasn't meant to be.*

Sorry. I know this sounds harsh.

I know if you care about someone, and you are hoping they will love you, that you want me to say, "I can help make that happen for you."

The truth is, I *can* help you.

I *can* help you make the relationship better, closer, and even get a second chance. But I *can't* help you make someone love you if they aren't *meant* to.

But that's okay. I assure you, we have all thought, at one time or another, that the person we are fixated on NOW *is* the only one.

If you don't have a love partner in your life right now, you will. You can't miss with love, for love is a destiny that we are all given. If love seems to not be present, believe that the pieces are falling into place so that the right person can merge with you.

One of the best ways to ensure that love shows up in your life, is to love yourself first. Do this by taking care of you.

I don't mean to go get all narcissistic and greedy and unthoughtful. I mean, make sure you feel good before you proceed in anything. Honor your feelings. By doing this, you show love to yourself.

Only let love and loving people around you. Begin to move out and away from low frequency people that make you feel bad or less than all you can be. Love doesn't hurt. Love emboldens and expands you into a 'better you.' Sometimes it doesn't move as fast as you like because love is a force all its own.

Be assured, love is coming for you too.

Love has its own timing and its own plan. Love is divine and perhaps God *is* love. Rest assured, love will find you.

The truth is, Natalie did manage to have her ex boyfriend show up in her life and be with him that last time. And that was the last time that she saw him, because they never did end up reconciling.

The moral of the story, and what we all can take away from this is: You can manifest something in the moment, but you can't manifest somebody having feelings for you that they don't really have.

As I said, love is a divine force and thus, is often out of our hands.

In the end, Natalie didn't get the relationship that she wanted with her ex boyfriend. But she did get to see him one more time, and that did bring her some sense of closure and happiness.

Plus, of course she got the satisfaction of knowing that she can manifest things she wants, even the seemingly impossible.

That said, rules are made to be broken and goodness knows, in love, anything goes. So yes, you can get someone excited to see you, and yes you can most likely get the date you want with someone, but making them fall in love with you? Well, I'd pray!

Delightfully, Natalie's story does have a happy ending.

A year later, Natalie met Troy, who *is* the man of her dreams. They are happily married today, and wow, is she happy it didn't work out with her ex!

If you don't see how love could happen for you, guess what? You don't need to see it. It's coming for you, as much as you are looking for it.

As hard as love may feel for you now, try and have faith.

Stay happy and expecting.

Remember how great it was for Natalie that her wish for the wrong man *wasn't* granted!

CHAPTER 4

Decide What To Wish For

After about five years of manifesting for myself, and helping my clients manifest, I found myself at a standstill. I realized I was on glide. I didn't know what I wanted, and because of that, I wasn't manifesting anything new in my life.

I felt stuck.

I realized that very often, one of the hardest things about manifesting is deciding what you really want, and getting excited about it.

This is because it's the excitement and love and passion for the thing that drives it towards you.

We manifest things in our life that we love.

Thus, even though this may seem very simple and obvious at

first, we begin with the first step on our way to making our dream a reality, and the first step of our 5 step process, which is deciding what to wish for.

Step 1 – Decide What to Wish For.

The first step toward manifesting your dream is figuring out just what really gets you excited, passionate, and in love enough to manifest it!

There will be no lukewarm manifestations!

You manifest things you love.

Figuring out what really makes you happy and what you *really* love might be the hardest part of the entire process of manifestation.

Oh, you think that won't be so hard, huh?

You say you're busting out with desires, ready to go?

We'll, okay, let's try it...

Let me ask you now, "What makes your heart sing?"

Hmm. Did she just say, "sing"?

Well, yes I did.

Okay, I'm listening.

What is it that you could bring into your life

that would truly make your spirit and your heart happy?

Did you get stuck on that one?

Perhaps, did you stop yourself from believing you could get it? Or, is it that other than paying the bills and your daily responsibilities, you couldn't put your finger on something you really wanted just for you?

Let's go there. If you're really in a topsy-turvy place, can't pay your bills or find any security, then the first thing you're going to want to manifest is abundance, security, safety, and contentment.

These are valid wishes.

Survival is first in the paradigm of importance.

However, if you are getting along fine, and who wants to be just fine? — You want total BLISS! — I'm trying to push you into manifesting something amazing!

When we were children, we had no problem figuring out what we wanted.

Our dreams didn't get squashed. We just kept dreaming bigger and bigger.

Somewhere along the line, we got told not to dream so big, or that it would be impossible to buy a castle, for instance. (My best friend's brother actually owns a castle in Ireland, so it's *not* impossible.)

It's impossible to become a movie star (Did it. Okay, maybe 'star' wouldn't be quite the right word, but I *did* get paid to be in movies.)

It's impossible, unless you're rich, to travel the world (but I'm currently doing that too).

We tell ourselves it's impossible and we end up believing we can't attain our dreams.

Inevitably, we stop trying to get our wishes and we stop believing.

Believing it's impossible, we then stop wanting, dreaming, and wishing. And then we don't get anything.

Then our worst fears are realized

because we are living un-magical lives.

If you were truly satis?ed with just paying your bills, going to work, and muddling through the rat race, then you wouldn't be reading this.

I can assure you that you will never have that life again. Miracles and magic do still exist, and you're about to tap into them. It's going to make you *so* happy!

I don't want to drone on about my own life, but for some of you, it may prove helpful to hear some real life examples of the use of this and how it flows. Hence, I'm going to share one of my first manifestations, one that occurred when I first starting using this process consciously.

Looking back, I realize how important being very precise is, when you send out your desires. If you wanted to call me, you would call 'Linda West.' If you dialed up 'Laura West,' you would be close, but you still wouldn't get *me* on the phone.

It's the same exact thing with manifesting.

This is why, as we move along, I will continue to drum it into you, to be *precise* about what you want.

In this case study, I received exactly what I dialed up.

Date/Time/Event. I advise you to do the same; the more exact, the better.

I had just started working with other people teaching this 5-step process and I was lecturing on my first book about frequencies.

At the time, my son was five years old, I was recently divorced, and didn't have much money.

I could barely pay the electric bill. And yes, those rock and roll riches-to-rags stories are true.

This was previous to *The Secret,* so there wasn't much of a market for people interested in learning frequency attunement, or what later would be popularly known as 'The Law of Attraction.'

Despite the difficulties I was having just bringing up

a child alone in uber expensive LA, I still found myself really wanting to learn how to surf. The ocean just thrilled me.

I was a Buffalo girl and we only had rivers and lakes.

The ocean was passionate, wild, and mysterious. I couldn't believe those Californians were just riding all over it on surfboards!

I fell in love with surfing and the ocean. I took lessons, I watched videos, and I floundered around in the waves as best I could.

I wanted so much to learn how to surf but I just couldn't seem to get it. I was a gymnast my whole life so it was darn right humiliating that I couldn't master even beginner moves on my surfboard. Of course, in a gym you don't have sharks or waves that can kill you. What a thrill! :)

When I got into the water, wow, the Paci?c was really cold and the big crowds made me feel insecure. I just couldn't seem to learn and get good.

I avidly watched all the Roxy videos of the girls in bikinis in

Hawaii at Waikiki, surfing in front of Diamond Head. They looked so happy, smiling, jumping in the water with their warm little suits on, and making it look so fun and easy!

That's when my wish was born.

Hawaii was my answer to conquering surfing. I wanted to learn to surf in Hawaii just like the girls in the Roxy video!

Of course, a trip to Hawaii is not cheap and so at the time not in my budget at all. I was talking to my 'then' boyfriend and he said, "Why don't you try and manifest this with the techniques you use with your clients?"

Big Duh!

All right. The game was on! We decided to try manifesting the trip together (even though he didn't really *love* surfing. He just wanted to go to Hawaii — valid enough).

We picked out the perfect date and gave ourselves a month until the end of October, because that's when the crowd thinned and the water was still warm. Okay, so far, so good.

I was pretty new at 'wish manifesting' *consciously*, so I didn't know what to expect. As most people would think, I thought some magical money would appear that I didn't know about. Falling from the sky when I needed it most...

Alas, no sudden windfall of vacation cash came in that month.

I continued to watch my surf videos, fake practicing along on my carpet, and putting out good vibes. I really didn't think about our wish until it hit the end of October.

My boyfriend (smirkingly) said to me, "I guess your 'manifesting stuff' doesn't work. You didn't manifest the trip and you didn't manifest the *money* to take the trip."

I looked at the calendar and the date hit me. There it was, the last day of October circled in bright red flare, and there was no trip in sight.

The truth of it was glaring at me in red, almost sad, now positioned right next to my favorite surf poster of the Roxy girls surfing happily on Waikiki's beautiful perfect waves.

I was kind of disappointed and thought, "Well, all right. Maybe I did something wrong or maybe the technique wasn't right."

I certainly had enough enthusiasm and love for it, and that's the most powerful attractor.

I had certainly manifested many other darn right unbelievable things before so I knew it was possible.

I believed.

In any case I didn't get all bent out of shape about it.

Remember when I told you that when your wish is granted it often shows up in an unusually delightful way you never would have thought of? That surprise delivery aspect is actually one of the coolest parts about the whole wish thing coming true!

You understand you don't have to know how, you just have to believe it will...

You understand the magic of life and the divine design working. That is worth a thousand dream vacations and wads of cash because it is the source of true happiness, which is *connection*.

Wholeness. Unity. One.

I really meant that, and sometimes it's as good as getting what you wish for, as you will see!

Continuing on, *remember that this happened to me, and this is a completely true story.*

It's Halloween morning. The last day of October . . . the 31st is circled in red. I'm staring at it mocking me, when I receive a phone call.

It was from a former client that I had known when I worked at the rehab. (I had a short stint as a spiritual counselor at a 'la dee da' Malibu star rehab.)

The former client, Ruby, told me that she had relapsed and hurt herself and her daughter had found her. (Ruby had a bad alcohol problem and had been battling it on and off for years.) Ruby's best friend, after finding out about the drunken incident, had gotten so upset that she took the daughter to her house and refused to let her go back home until Ruby went back to rehab.

(This best friend may or may not have been a famous 80s rock star but I can't really say..:)

Fair enough.

The problem was that Ruby and her daughter had a special family vacation planned and they were all packed and ready to go. There was no time for a rehab visit.

What were they to do?

Hmmm. And this is how it flows folks.

This is how one person's problem needing to be solved

merged with the manifestation of my wish being granted.

This is close to the exact conversation that ensued:

Ruby said, "I really need your help Linda. I totally screwed up and drank. I know it's last minute, but xyz has taken my daughter and won't give her back to go on our trip unless she knows for sure I won't drink. If I pay for everything, can you please go with us to Hawaii tomorrow *all-expenses-paid,* and be my sober coach?"

She continued on to explain that, "My daughter and I have signed up for surf lessons all week so I hope you're up for that. We're staying right in Waikiki..."

Gee, I had to think long and hard on that one!

I packed my bags and surfboard and we left the next day!

The next day, November 1, I was surfing in the warm waves of Waikiki.

I was surfing *exactly* in the same place as the girls in my Roxy 'learn to surf' video.

(I wasn't surfing anything like the girls in the video but I was there doing my best and happy as a clam!)

That's how I learned to surf in Waikiki.

For free.

How cool, right???!

Surfing has since become one of the greatest joys of my

life. I still surf all the time. It still reigns as one of my happiest and favorite manifestations and it gives me great muscles too.

Remember if I can do it, you can do it.

This is my story, but you'll be telling your own stories soon because this works for everyone.

If you love it you will manifest it, and I can help you.

Unfortunately, the ex-boyfriend did not manifest Hawaii.

I can only assume he wasn't excited or nearly as much in *love* with the idea of surfing as I was.

The universe brought it to me, but he stayed home. He did not get to learn to surf and he did not get the tan, but he did get to learn a powerful message about the laws of manifestation.

Moving along, darlings. Let's go get you what you want!

Now it's your turn to manifest your dreams.

So, what kinds of dreams do you have locked inside of you? What kinds of fantasies?

What kinds of wishes and what kinds of joys are just waiting to be released and sprung into your life?

Because people do have so much resistance to even

finding out what they really love and what would make them happy, I developed this simple exercise to help you.

Please take a moment to try this now and then afterwards write down everything that you get.

Step 1 exercise – Figuring out what you want.

1. Sit down in a quiet place and take three deep breaths, one for mind, one for body, and one for spirit.

2. When you are comfortable and relaxed I want you to:

Imagine...

You were just given $300 million dollars as a gift.

Now, check in with your triangle. Ask your mind what it wants to do with $300 million dollars. Ask your body what it wants to do with $300 million dollars.

Now ask your heart and spirit what dream it wants to follow with the freedom allowed by that $300 million dollars?

Now that you have all the money in the world.

What DO YOU want?

CHAPTER 5

The Triangle Check

How did you do with your exercise?

Did wishes and ideas pour in, or did you find a dry well?

Even after years of manifesting, you will find that you still have to dig to find out what really makes your heart soar. You just can't coast through life. Change enlivens and rejuvenates you.

You must learn, stretch, and grow toward bliss.

Joy is not stagnant; it is a force and a flow. Like a river, , in order to experience true happiness, you must run and rejoin all of yourself as a creator.

Just as I recommended to you, I urged myself to 'create' my life instead going on autopilot.

I used the same sample question below to help me to identify what I really wanted next in my life.

As I instructed you to do, I sat down I took a few breaths and imagined what I would do if I had $300 million.

Every so often, we need a boost to start dreaming again. Life gets in the way of joy sometimes.

What if I did have that elusive trust fund from my Uncle Buffet or I hit the lottery? Oh, the power of *"what if I had $300 million dollars"* — then what? If the world's the limit, what in the world *do I really want?*

Now, this sounds so rudimentary, I know, but don't discount it because it sounds so obvious!

Having a true passion for something is the only way to make

it real.

My beginning thoughts went like this:

First of all, I would buy the rainforest to protect it and send a bunch of money to charities I care about.

I would take care of the people in my life that need help, a home, or need support or a car, or whatnot, and I would buy that for them....but then I'm going to have several millions leftover. So then, what about just for me?

You think that would be easy. You'll see later that it's one of the hardest and most important parts to successful manifesting!

What I came up with was that I didn't care about owning a yacht or a mansion or anything like that. I wanted experiences!

I wanted to go touch everything in the world!

I wanted to see all the far away lands I'd heard about!

I wanted to meet unique people!

I wanted see different exotic places!

I wanted to try new things and I wanted to see the world!

Wow, *now* I was excited!

Excitement is the biggest key in manifesting.

When you get excited, it means you're having joyful feelings about it coming true.

Feelings are the little motors that create the vibrations that manifest for you.

Those excitement feelings are exactly what we are looking for!

I realized what I *really* wanted to manifest, was traveling around the world.

When I checked in with myself, I found out that I had no resistance to traveling. Every bit of me wanted to experience all of these different places around the globe.

The only thing I didn't have was money. Ha ha. Now I know that seems like a large part of the puzzle piece missing. But as you'll see, *that* part we can manifest.

The next day, a girlfriend of mine, Andrea, walked into my restaurant and she was glowing.

I asked her what was new and she explained to me that she had just come back from being on a new TV show that was like "Survivor," and she had been in a far-away place doing exotic, interesting things.

I was so stoked that my friend had just walked in and said she'd just done exactly what I wanted to manifest for myself. On top of it, she won money?

I gushingly said, "Oh my gosh, Andrea, that's exactly what I was wishing for too! I want to be able to travel and see exotic sites and do something unique like that. It sounds amazing!"

She looked at me kind of oddly and then she took my hand and said, "Oh Linda, I can make that happen for you. I know the producers. I can get you on the next show!"

I was floored!

I had been reluctant to say anything about my own great desires, but if I hadn't, what would have happened?

She would have had her coffee and a nice chat about the weather and off she would have gone.

Instead, my love for the adventure of it all blurted out of me and here was my wish being answered!

In less than 24 hours of my identifying what would really make me happy and excited, in walked the answer to my dream coming true!

...or so I thought.

Very often, we get a sign before we get the manifestation, as in this case.

Sometimes the universe has to put into action the bigger plan before your wish can manifest. You will often get little symbols or hints of your desire manifesting before it actually occurs.

In this case, my friend was just a symbol of what was about to come into my life, as far as traveling the world.

(But I'll save that story for last) :)

I identified this wish a month ago, and now my wish has come true.

I'm in the middle of living that wish now and sharing how I manifested that with you *while* I'm actually in the reality of that wish coming true.

I write this for you now so that you will know that it's going to be a surprise! Wishes truly are 'kissed' by the divine because they show up as gifts. Not just what you wanted, but tied with a beautiful special bow, to let you know that the angels brought it to you.

I didn't know how my wish to travel the world was going to come through, and you won't know how it's going to come through either. All I can assure you, my dear friends, is that *it will come* in a beautiful, amazing way.

I teach my clients this technique because I love people, and I want you to help yourself and to help everyone you love to have a better life.

Maybe you need better health. Maybe you need more than a trip. Maybe you need a miracle.

I really believe any kind of miracle is possible with this technique because you're tapping into God, and as a child of God, we have access to the divine powers of God when they're used in divine ways.

Dealing With the Three Judges

Now that you have figured out what you love and want to manifest, we have to go see the judges.

You have to be clear about what you want.

The reason you have to be clear is because you will not manifest what you want unless *all of three parts of you* want it.

Meaning that, sometimes we shut out voices we don't want to hear — but they are trying to communicate with us.

In the *West,* we tend to listen primarily to our mind, and not as much to the voice of our bodies or our spirit hearts.

What we manifest always depends on an agreement between the three parts that make up our whole in the third dimension.

Very often, you will find that some part of your triangle of judges wants to take smaller steps than the other parts. This means a part of you is unsure.

Don't fight that.

That voice is protecting you and looking out for an integral part of your happiness.

As much as you want to leap straight into your dream, sometimes steps towards it are better.

The Beauty of Taking Steps

Sometimes a dream takes steps. It takes steps, not because you can't immediately manifest it, but because we are humans. The truth is, change is scary to most humans.

Big leaps mean big cajones.

Your life changes when *things* change.

Things change when *you* change.

These are things you might not be so ready to change yet, but that must be moved to allow your wish to come in.

Sometimes that means changing jobs, sometimes friends,

sometimes marriages....

Even when those things that we change are for the better, it can still be scary.

That's why I encourage you to take steps.

Take steps towards what you want.

Manifest and re-access.

How do you feel?

If the rush is on, take another step towards manifesting your wish.

If the thrill is gone, go with it...

You're over it. You got it and it stinks.

Great. You didn't change your whole world to figure out you were going in a direction that doesn't make you happy!

I was so happy because I manifested winning a big news reporter contest. As a result I was offered a position as an anchorwoman on the show that I really admired.

Not only was I happy for the job, but come on, the wish coming true thing was just AWESOME!

I went to Austin, Texas to look for a place to live and I was psyched. I was ready to pull up all my roots from California and move fully into my new life as a news reporter on a big show.

However, when I started working at the news office, I felt awful. I hated it.

I liked my team but the rest of it just wasn't for me.

I packed up and went home.

I was going in the wrong direction for my ultimate happiness and I was not going to keep walking one more minute once I knew that.

Yes, I had manifested what I wanted, but once I got it, I realized it wasn't going to make me happy. So I changed my mind.

Thus, you see the beauty of taking steps.

Sometimes you think you want something, and then you get it, and you realize you were wrong.

I took a step. I rented a place for a month to check it out. I didn't pack up and move my whole life. It was no effort to go back and reassess what I really wanted next.

Learning what you don't want is a great way to point you toward what you really *do* want. Once you know what you don't want, you have another piece of the puzzle to what you really need to make yourself happy all the way through.

One of the ways to make sure you don't waste time going toward something you don't really want, is to check in with your triangle.

I call this my TRIANGLE CHECK.

When you go to manifest something, you need to realize that you're working with three parts of yourself.

Three little judges, if you will — we have our own little 'congressional system' and balancing act going on.

In our case, it's the mind, the body, and the spirit.

Whether you like it or not, you must pay attention to what each one of them is saying.

The fact is, you won't manifest anything or pull it into the third dimension without all three parts of yourself agreeing on it.

Ultimately, you are using six-dimensional geometry to do this, so that it can manifest.

In my practice, very often my clients get in their own way, because they don't really want what they're trying to manifest!

As I said, all three parts of you have to agree, and *I meant it.* The most likely reason somebody is not manifesting something in their life that they truly seem to

want, is because a part of them is blocking it.

All three parts of you have a voice, and a choice in what you create. You can't ignore any part of you.

Here's an example from one of my lectures where a pretty young woman named Helen raised her hand and waved it about furiously, saying she really needed help.

She claimed she wanted to marry a handsome, well-dressed young man in her office. She knew if she could just learn how to manifest correctly, that dream would be a reality and she'd be walking down the aisle with him.

She was obviously enthusiastic! Helen's hand had been the first one that shot up when I asked for a volunteer.

Enthusiasm is a good start.

She was seemingly very sure of her attraction and similarity to this man.

Best yet, she was at a lecture on 'How to Learn to Manifest.' I had no doubt that this young woman would be able to manifest things in her life!

However, marrying somebody she didn't know? I had some questions.

I had to take this wish of hers to her judges to get a true call.

What would we find when we did a basic *Triangle Check?*

My very first questions to Helen quickly identified that she'd never dated this guy in the office, and in fact had barely had a conversation with him at work. Again, she reiterated to me how much she thought he was handsome and smart, and from across the room, she just knew he was 'the *one.*'

Okay, sounds like she knew what she wanted, but then what was the next logical question? She never had a date with this guy, so she didn't really know him and maybe he was not a good guy at all (i.e., he could be a real jerk, a loser, a gambler, or a player); maybe he just *looks* good!

As I tried to get to exactly what she wanted, I realized we still needed to be more clear.

I asked the next logical question (the same way I suggest you ask yourself the next logical questions about your wish).

The next obvious question I asked her was, "Are you sure that marriage is what you want? Is this large, lifetime-committed step, with a person you don't really know, what you really want now? All of you?"

Let's take this to our congressional system and take a look at it from there, shall we?

Now, it sounded as if she was very certain on a *BODY* level that she was very attracted to this man.

Okay, so far so good. We have one part that thinks he's the cat's meow — on the body level then, it appears to be a full go.

Okay, moving along, let's continue by checking in with the Spirit.

How does the *SPIRIT* feel about this *marrying the co-worker* wish?

From what I was getting, her spirit thinks he's attractive and was excited about getting to know him. However, it appears that her *SPIRIT* also feels marrying somebody that she doesn't really know, and could end up being completely wrong for her (or worse yet, horribly

suffocating to her true calling) is absurd.

You can see why the spirit can't really get on board with

Helen manifesting the marrying of this man.

Now the wish is starting to sound frivolous and not so perfect.

Let's continue around the triangle and check into what her *MIND* has to say about her marrying somebody with whom she's never even had a long conversation.

My assumption is her mind will be saying things like,

"Hello, are you crazy? There is no way we are going to allow you to manifest this! You've never gone out with him! We may have no compatibility, he might be boring, or he might be bad in bed. Hell no! Hey, you might not even want to be his *girlfriend*, let alone his *wife*!"

As you can see, her mind is going to have a problem with this.

Her mind is not going to go along with her taking a huge leap into marriage with somebody she does not know.

Let's sum up our triangle check.

The results go like this —

The *BODY* is full in with a *YES*.

The *SPIRIT* and *MIND* both say a big *NO*.

So guess what?

Right.

She's not going to manifest marrying this guy at this moment. What is the grand lesson here?

Make sure you check in with your triangle,

mind, body and spirit.

They had better agree

or manifestation you won't see.

Twiddle dee dee and twiddle dee dum.

Helen was finally able to discover that she was really *not* ready to marry this guy.

In fact, she wasn't ready to marry *any* guy!

When she got really honest with herself and listened to what all parts of her triangle were voicing, she wasn't really even comfortable having a full date with him!

So, what did she find when she listened to her triangle core about what all three parts of her would be comfortable and happy about manifesting *right now*?

A simple cup of coffee.

In the end, all three parts of her were really only excited about moving forward with a simple cup of coffee with him!

Bingo! All three parts of her were excited about going out to coffee with this handsome guy in her office.

What a perfect and natural next step.

She found the exact thing she was ready for and really excited about. Now the rest was going to be simple. Now that all three parts of her were excited about it, we could use the 5-step process.

I can't say I was surprised when I heard back from Helen later that month. She had already had that cup of coffee she had decided to manifest, and was looking forward to a date with her office crush that Saturday night.

My friends, if I can do it, she can do it, we can do it, *you* can do it!

As soon as you realize it's really all about *you*.

And once you are being clear about you, then you can create anything.

Get to know all sides of you.

Then you'll start to see things materialize overnight, like magic. When you truly grasp the concept that most of the time the little devil keeping you away from your dreams, and sometimes in a victim or unhealthy place, is of your own making, then you must also realize that you have the ability to change it.

Get clear, choose well, and manifest it into your world.

It is that simple.

Because so many new students get hung up on this part of the manifestation process, I want to make sure you understand.

Here's another example of the use of the triangle for clarity, from my private practice.

George came to see me about something he wanted to manifest. George worked for a huge corporation and was stuck in middle management. George wanted to manifest becoming the CEO of the company.

Now, this isn't a huge jumping wish that is impossible.

It could very well happen! Having worked in my lectures with many people who are trying to make their wishes come true, I knew that a common mistake people made was trying to wish for something way bigger than what they were actually ready for. So I had questions for George.

Knowing this is a common mistake, and something that held people back, I quizzed him to get him into true clarity. I used the triangle process with George to make sure he was ready for this big wish.

I said, "Okay, you want to manifest being a CEO. Are you sure?"

George said, "Yes. I really yearn to be the CEO. I want the money, I want the prestige, I want the big office, and the big title."

I kept quizzing him on this because I knew from experience

that leaping from the middle to the CEO is difficult.

This is not because you can't do it through manifestation,

but because all three parts of your triangle usually are

not ready for that much of a huge change at once.

I've talked about the human condition and its need for small steps.

Continuing on, I asked him more questions.

"So you want to be the head honcho?"

George nodded, and I continued, "So you are all ready to work 12 to 14 hours a day and travel the world, like a CEO of such a big company would need to do?"

This is when he began to hesitate and that's when I knew he had wished too big. He was already starting to resist his own wish!

I told you we do this!

Once George took a moment to actually think about that reality of being a CEO everyday, the 14-hour workday, away from home often with business travel....

He said, "Oh well, I have two small children at home so I couldn't work that long or really travel that much. No, I wouldn't like that part of the job."

Then I had to say to George, "But that *is* the job of a

CEO, George. Those are the hours and the requirements."

If you want the job, then those things will be part of your life, because those things go along with the job of the CEO."

Now things were starting to take on a different color.

Now George really had to stop and wonder what he had been wishing for, and what he really wanted. I told him to go back and check inside himself for the truth.

Run the *Triangle Check*.

When George did check in with his three inside judges, what he found was a big *no* from his heart, and a big *no* from his spirit.

His mind was the only one excited about being a CEO and it was only his mind's voice that was making the wish. His mind reasoned that his life would be better if he ran the company and made more money for his family.

And why wouldn't George think this? We are often told to go for the top, grab the money, sell your life to the man…We can get programmed to move toward things we don't even really want.

You owe it to yourself to be kind enough to honor all parts of yourself and make yourself happier!

As I continued to ask questions of George to help him

gain clarity, other things were revealed.

He didn't want to be away from his children and wife for long hours every day. He wanted to be part of his children's lives and sports teams, and he enjoyed bowling and golfing with his wife. However, if he was made CEO, his family and friends would all be put on the back burner while he ran this huge company.

This is a *BODY* feeling being voiced, involving family and home. His wish was not going to make his body axis happy at all! This was a family guy, and his family was important to him.

Upon more examination, we found that George's *SPIRIT* wasn't thrilled about working 14 hours a day for a company he didn't love either. George had hobbies and interests that he enjoyed outside of work, and all the time devoted to work

would mean they would suffer.

When George did check in, this was the end result:

Body — No

Spirit — No

Mind — Yes

(but programmed?)

Total — No

Once again, we discovered that a person really didn't want what they were wishing for once they really looked at it.

Much like Helen, once we were able to truly get a clear message after using the *Triangle Check*, we could move ahead to manifest.

When we finally whittled it down to what George *really* wanted, all he *really* wanted was more *money*. He also wanted more creativity with room for advancement.
That's it!

51

George didn't really want the $1 million job, he didn't need the title of CEO, and he didn't want a career that would pretty much take over his whole life. He just wanted *more*.

Once we were able to figure out what he really wanted, we could manifest it. Now there would be no more resistance to that wish coming true.

Now let's take your wish and put it through the same check with your inner judges.

Exercise 2 - The Triangle Check

Based on these client stories, let's take a look at what you're wishing for!

Take a moment to check in with your triangle. How do you feel? How does your body *feel* about it? How does your head *think* about it? How does your spirit *feel* about it coming true? Is there any resistance? Are all three parts of you ready for this *now*?

Ask yourself some questions and try to pinpoint the truth for yourself. Ask questions like I asked of George and Helen.

Can you scale it down in any way, where you feel more comfortable?

CHAPTER 6

Getting into a High Frequency

So how are YOU feeling?

Are you ready to move ahead with your wish?

Are you so ready, that if it came to you tomorrow, you'd be totally happy about it?

If you truthfully answer *yes*, then you're ready.

Good, because we are going to go manifest it and sometimes it happens right away.

In my experience, I very often have seen things manifest within 24 hours.

Then conversely, at other times, it takes a little while to manifest because the pieces have to be put into place.

In this case, signs will show up to show you that the message has been received.

Step 1: You've identified what you wanted and made sure that all three parts of you are in agreement.

We are ready to move on to Step 2 in the process of creation, getting yourself in a high frequency..

To manifest quickly, you need to get *yourself into the highest frequency possible.*

Like attracts like.

Good things come in on good vibrations.

To manifest the quickest, stay in the highest frequency possible — all the time.

Do you know what a high frequency is?

High frequency is any time you're feeling good, like when you hear birds singing, or little kids laughing, whenever love is emanating from you, or you're bouncing off the walls with joy.

High frequencies are what you want in your life.

Simply put, the higher the frequency, the more divine, happy, and good it feels.

The science of frequencies can get kind of complicated, but to simplify things, just remember that high frequencies make you feel good, so you should always move toward them.

Move toward things that make you feel good.

Conversely, low frequencies make you feel bad.

Examples of low frequencies are: getting sick, gaining weight, losing your job, and mean people.

Whenever you identify a low frequency, you should move away from it.

The way you move away from low frequencies is – well, if it's your mother-in-law, you can walk out the door, but vibrationally, you can do that by raising your frequency above it — by going to the *next highest frequency* you can get to.

If the science of frequencies interests you, then you should check out my first book, where I go into the complete understanding of the Science of Frequencies and the Law of Attunement, <u>Ultimate Power</u>.

The next simple part of frequencies you need to understand is how frequencies interact with each other.

Similar frequencies are drawn to other

frequencies like themselves.

Like attracts like.

Like frequencies attract like frequencies by the Law of Attraction.

To sum it up, everything has a frequency, but what we are looking for are the *high frequencies — the frequencies that make you feel good.*

It's very important to launch a high-frequency wish or goal off of *another* high-frequency vibration.

Don't go practicing this technique when you're in fear, doubt, sadness, or illness!

You have to wait until you get into an authentically happy place, or somehow boost yourself into a *fake* happy place, which also counts as a high frequency.

What you're feeling is what you're feeling. It doesn't matter how you got there.

Now we may do the exercise on manifesting.

Because of the Law of Affinity, remember to Make-A-Wish when you're in a high frequency!

A few years ago, I was in Big Sur. I was on a big tree swing in front of my friend's cottage. The swing was one of the coolest things I'd ever been. It swung way out over the road below and overlooked the Paci?c ocean.

Every time I would swing out over the roadway, people driving by would look up and be totally surprised to see me, looking as if I had fallen out of the sky. They would wave up and break out in smiles as I appeared suddenly in the clouds above them.

This for some reason made me ecstatically happy and joyful.

The whole child-like hiding, then popping through the clouds and surprising people driving by on the road was so fun to me!

I realized at that moment of silly joy, "Hello Linda, this is Make-A-Wish time!"

Obviously, the goofy swing thing was a hoot for me, but you have to find what pops you into a higher vibe.

And why was it the perfect time? To recap:

I was so ecstatically happy, I was hitting a very high frequency. When you are in a high frequency, it is the time to send out your wishes. A high frequency means it's Make-A-Wish time.

When high vibes are ringing in your head, that's the right time to Make-A-Wish.

If you remember nothing else from this book, every time you get in a super happy place remember it's wish time — so send out those wishes baby!

As you'll see, like attracts like, by the Law of Affinity, but it's what we *FEEL* that creates the vibrations that set up the pattern for the light vibrations to integrate with.

We feel things into existence in the third dimension.

We build a foundational house for the dream to manifest by *'loving it'* to ourselves with a high frequency.

Ultimately, we're talking about Source key energy that you want to match up with, or emulate.

I found one of the easiest, sure?re ways of getting into a high frequency is to read a comedy or watch a comedy. When you're laughing, you're officially in a high frequency. Then, while you're laughing... (it's *go* time!)

I also walk in nature or do something artistic to get myself into a high frequency. If I'm not feeling up, a sure?re way to raise my frequency is a hot yoga class.

Begin to look around in your life, and find what brings you joy. Become aware of when you enter those special high-frequency moments.

When you have identified, without a doubt, that you're

in a high frequency and it's Make-A-Wish time, then it's time to move on to Step 3 and make that wish to the universe in the form of a movie.

CHAPTER 7

How to make your Make-A-Wish movie

Now that you've done Step 1, and you are able to identify what you want, and you've done Step 2 and you are in a *Make-A-Wish* high frequency, you can move on to Step 3 — making a *Make-A-Wish* movie.

Wherever you are, excuse yourself for a moment, or if you're alone in a high frequency, then you are ready to go.

This step involves making up a *movie* in your head with real players. Imagine what you think everybody would be saying if your dream were true NOW — in the present.

Imagine what you are *hearing*, the natural conversation that is taking place as this dream materializes, and what you and people around you are *saying*.

Most importantly, you must imagine how you would really *really* feel if your wish came true now. Like if a genie in the bottle suddenly appeared and said, "Go. Wish number 1 — poof!" There is your dream, right there in your hands – how would you feel?

Feel it. Feel the joy of it. Feel the wonder of it. Feel it!

If you're creating the movie realistically, some things you might naturally be feeling are joy, awe, gratitude and thinking, "Hooray! My wish is coming true right now!"

Your goal is to create such a believable movie inside your head, by using as many senses and creativity as possible, *that you actually start to get excited about it, as if it were real.*

You actually attempt to fake yourself out.

You fake yourself into a feeling by creating a movie exactly as you'd like to see it playing out in your life. You *play act,* to the point that you get excited about the possibility of it, and the truth of it.

When you actually feel excited or happy, your movie has been successful!

Now that you are feeling the realness of it, try to hold

onto that feeling of *as if* for as long as possible.

Attempt to hold the feeling of it actually occurring, and the joy

you feel from it, for as long as possible.

> The science on this says that you need exactly 16 seconds to send out a frequency wave. Your goal is to feel that fake feeling of accomplishment and getting what you want -- for 16 seconds or more...

As you're creating this movie inside you, what you're actually doing is creating and sending out a vibrational pattern that you want *matched by the universe* (i.e., the Law of Attraction, the Law of Affinity, Like Attracts Like, etc.)

In this movie, you need to use all parts of yourself. It's very important that you use all of your senses to make this make-believe movie.

Imagine it in the exact way you want it to happen. Imagine what it would look like if this little miracle were coming true and it was taking place in your life right now.

Most likely, the scenario you're creating is going to have other players, and it will probably involve people saying things to you like, "Congratulations! You finally got the promotion," or "...That's wonderful! That girl is on the phone for you," or "... There's somebody at the door who wants to talk to you about giving you that school grant."

It's going to be a fake movie that you make up, only it's the movie you want to see take place in your life.

It should consist of the actions and thoughts you would be *hearing*, the sights and people you would be *seeing*, and most importantly, what you would be *feeling* if it were coming true right *now. . .*

In the present.

I like to get in a private place and then close my eyes, and imagine it just like a little Hollywood movie.

Here's an example from one of my lectures and one of the people that I was working with whom I mentioned earlier.

Helen was the young woman who wanted to marry the guy

who worked in her of?ce. Let's use her as an example.

We used the *Triangle Check* and we got her wish narrowed down to exactly what Helen wanted. (Step 1)

Next we were going to move her into a high frequency (Step 2), and then we will create her *Make-A-Wish* movie (Step 3).

I first wanted to talk to Helen a bit about love and being careful about manifesting love. In this case, a cup of coffee seems innocent enough, but you need to know that you have to be careful when you're manifesting things about or with other people.

You may send out enchanting thoughts about yourself and vibrations. Then, if that person is enchanted by you, it's their free will if they decide to pursue you.

What you cannot do is force people to do things, nor can you use this in an evil way.

You can't manifest anything from the lower realms, which are dark, and secondly, you have Karma to contend with, and in my experience — *Karma is a bitch.*

Okay. Well, this conversation was a dual success. Not only did Helen get clarification on manifesting and wishing for love, she also started laughing. Of course, as soon as she was laughing, that signaled *Make-A-Wish* time!

Usually, I have to tell a bad joke to get the person laughing, but this was perfect. So I began to work with her in real time, to coach her into her movie creation.

I said, "Okay, Helen, let's make a movie. This is how it happens. Now, close your eyes and tell me…What do you hear being said in your ears, if this were true and coming true right now? It might go like this: You're at your desk, the guy you like walks up to you, and he stops at your desk. Now, what might he say, if this were coming true?"

He might say something like, "Hello. How are you? You look pretty today. How about catching a cup of coffee after work?"

Then, how would you naturally respond?

You might say something like "Great! I'd love to go to coffee with you today. Thank you."

Then, how would you naturally feel?

You'd feel excited, overjoyed, and so happy that the guy you really like has just asked you out for coffee, which is what you really wanted to happen! Happiness!

Now your challenge is to keep that fake happiness going for 16 seconds.

I suggest adding another imaginary story to your initial story, change it up, and be creative.

Now bring up the movie inside your head again. Perhaps this time you're standing by the break room. Maybe he's coming by with a doughnut and coffee. It's time to begin a new dialogue. What might he say? And what might you say?

Add that into the movie. The more real you make it, the more real it becomes!

The most important part of the whole movie is the feeling that it creates in you. What you're feeling in your gut is the frequency maker, which drives your manifestation and pulls in your wish.

Feeling joy for something is the most important part. It's how we create things.

In this case, you are creating a fake feeling that will send out vibrations to pull in the *real thing*.

It is the art of believing as if it has already happened.

Some people will call this 'faith.'

Once you get into the feeling place, and you are feeling good and you're feeling excited, you will start to feel it slowly dissipate.

The fakeness will begin to show its ugly head. That's perfectly okay. That's normal.

We know that one of the keys to manifesting is how much energy (i.e., how much feeling) that we put into feeling *as if* it had just happened.

We can conclude logically then, that the longer we can keep the feelings going, the more likely it will appear.

And that leads us directly to Step 4!

CHAPTER 8

Calling in Your Best Friend

We have already identified the fact that the longer you keep a feeling going, the more power you put behind it. Those feelings create frequencies that are being sent out to find the matching frequencies (i.e., the stronger the frequency output, the stronger the attraction quality).

The next step involves *keeping* the feeling going.

Step 4 involves keeping the power of your *'as if'* feelings going *longer.*

We need to keep the feelings from the movie that you made up in your head (albeit the fake movie) revved up and powerful.

To keep these fake feelings motoring up, we're going to use a little trick I came up with to extend the feeling so you will have a stronger vibrational push.

This trick involves bringing in people that you love, who will be happy for you, if your wish comes true. Jesus mentions when two or more people pray together, that miracles happen. It's because the divine force joins them. I guess it's the holy trinity coming true, and once again we are dealing with the *triangle*.

Consequently, if you imagine that you're telling somebody *who really loves you* that your wish came true, and they connect to you, *in* your wish, then you will enact the divine force of the trinity, and it will join into *creating* your wish.

You may recall, I mentioned that things only manifest through the triangle, as in the mind, body, and spirit agreeing. So in this case, you're enacting a three-triangle force to help you manifest through feelings.

Mostly the feelings of *love*.

The movie gets you into the feeling of, "Wow, this is awesome! This is what it would be like if it were truly taking place."

As I mentioned,

> Your goal is to hold the fake feeling 'as if,' for as long as possible, at least 16 seconds.

As we know, this feeling will begin to dissipate, and when it does fade, this is when you imagine telling the story to somebody that you care about, someone who would be happy for you.

You are going to use all the tools you did in your Make-A-Wish movie.

This time, you are just making up a new story that involves you telling a friend that your wish came true.

Retell the story and, more importantly,
relive the happy feelings
and feel them.

You make the feelings feel real again for you. This creates the feelings again that create the waves you need to manifest.

Remember, *fake it till you make it!* Believe it before you get it. Like attracts like. Use that Law of Affinity!

For example, you might imagine telling your mother some great news. For instance, you received the promotion you were hoping for, you won the grant you were applying for, you got the date that you'd been hoping for, etc. Imagine telling your mother or your close friend —and how happy they are for you!

While you are imagining this, the feelings of their joy will combine with the feelings of your joy and rev up those feelings again, which will create more high frequencies.

Whoopeee!

Try to keep it going for 16 seconds.

At this point, maybe imagine telling *another* good friend, and how excited *they* will be for you, and how excited *you* will be, sharing the good news. And again, make it real. Use all your senses and extend those fake feelings!

Imagine what your best friend might be saying if the situation were real. She might say things like,

"Congratulations, this is awesome! I'm so proud of you, and I'm so happy for you…" And you might say, "Yeah, I know, I'm so happy too! I can hardly believe how lucky I am! This is the greatest day of my life!"

Bingo!

You are smack in the middle of creating those feeling frequencies that are ?owing out into the universe to get you those feelings for real. To get you what you want, for real, all that joy and success for real, the ability to tell that story for real, to the same real people, some day.

This is what creating your life is all about.

Do not just go every day into what is dealt to you like somebody on autopilot. Create your life. Make it happen the way *you want* it to happen. I know you can do it.

CHAPTER 9

Releasing to Receive

Okay darlings, we are rounding the bend to the last step and this truly is going to be the easiest.

To recap:

Step 1 -   We figured out what we really want.

Step 2 -   We got ourselves into a high frequency.

Step 3 -   We imagined a movie in our head that made it feel real.

Step 4 -   We extended those fake feelings by pretending to tell somebody we care about.

We've reached the final step.

Step 5 - Letting go with gratitude.

So here we are, at the end. You're about to manifest what you want. This last step involves letting go and being *grateful.*

It's very important to realize that things come in on frequency levels. So, your only job now is to stay away from any thoughts or worries that your manifestation might not come true.

You may focus on the love of it. When I wanted to learn to surf, I watched videos and had posters up, because I truly loved it.

I wasn't watching those videos to make it manifest more quick. I was watching those videos because I really,

really wanted to learn to surf.

The love of something manifests it to you quicker than anything. I'm trying to teach you how to fake the feeling of love for something, but it's not as good as the real thing.

When you can really fall in love or find a passion for something, that's the best yet.

Hello! Where's my stuff?

What if you've done all the steps and things still aren't showing up in your life?

So, this is where it gets a bit tricky, and you're going to have to really go with your gut on the truth of this.

If you're really jazzed and passionate about your dream coming true, but not *worried*, then that's the best place to be.

If you are in a hopeful and grateful place, and you're still waiting, then if you feel moved by spirit to do the process again, then *do it*.

At this point, if you feel really good, but just haven't seen anything show up, it is okay to quickly redo the exercises I just gave you.

If you're freaking out and afraid, and you think it's not working, then it's *not* working.

And your worrying is the *reason* it's not working.

I know it's a sad catch-22 situation to feel happy and grateful before it shows up, but that's how it goes.

It's best to stop fighting it and lean into it and do your best to combat your own inner demons (that like to doubt).

Our own inner healing is often highlighted as we move ahead to a higher-frequency life and way of being.

Your lower toxic issues will surface to challenge your newfound optimism and joy.

Expect them. Everyone has them. Just as everyone has a story that they could believe from their past, a story that can make it harder for them to expect anything good — or to accept anything good.

It's understandable that you are worried and fearful that something you really care about still seems so far away. You still have to fight those low frequencies if you want to see your dreams materialize.

This is inner work, but work you must do. Clean out those webs of despair and hopelessness and have faith.

Believe good things are meant for you and that you deserve them, because you do.

The more you learn to manifest, the more you will love yourself and be able to help and do things for others.

Everyone wins when you get strong and become a conscious creator of love and good things.

Worry is a low frequency. You need to let go, be cool, and go ahead with a divine nonchalance. Know that it is arriving in perfect time and stay in a grateful place as if it's already arrived.

Stay in a high frequency.

Your job is to get out of any low frequency of fear, and find a way to get back up into the high frequency of faith. This comes down to letting it go, and letting it come in, and being thankful for it, as if it has already happened.

Often when people really want something, they can't help but be concerned that it might not come in. Yet, this is the leap you have to take; it's called a 'leap of faith.'

You have to let it go and be grateful.

I think one of the most important parts of manifesting is being grateful and thankful.

I often thank God for things that I haven't seen show up in my life yet, as well as for the things that have shown up in my life.

In this way, I keep saying, "I have faith. You're bringing it in. I'm already grateful."

Appreciation — it's a good thing. It helps being grateful.

Not to mention being grateful is a very high frequency!

I can't say enough how staying in a high frequency is one of the surest ways to manifest quickly. Because of its importance, you must attend to your frequency level daily.

Some ways to accomplish raising your frequency are to: go out in nature, dance, play with pets, or watch a comedy.

Cultivate things that make you happy and bring you up to a good high-frequency feeling place.

The high frequencies always magnetize things to you more quickly.

A common question I get in my lectures is, "How long do I have to wait before my wish shows up?"

As I have said before, when you get very clear, and you really love something, and you don't have fear around it, and you are enthusiastic about it... then it can show up immediately. I've seen things show up within 24 hours, sometimes sooner.

Conversely, sometimes you have to wait for the divine order of things to fall into place.

Sometimes certain things in the universe, or people, have to be moved around and put into position in order for your wish to manifest. That can take time, especially if it involves other people. Then, you also have to deal with the timing of other people.

If what you want isn't manifesting right away, it just may be that the timing is not right.

I know it sounds cliché, but the universe works that way too.

Let's say you're not seeing your manifestation come through right away... as a hint, the first thing I would do is: Once I got into a high frequency, I would retry the whole five steps.

I would run through the process again and *send it out* again. Not in a stressful, fearful way, but just when I identified a high-frequency moment, I would send out another mini version of the wish.

The other thing I would do is go back and recheck

to make sure that I'm not wishing for something that's too big a step *for me* (according to my own triangle) .

Re-examine to see if there is any part of your wish that is giving you resistance.

Ask yourself, "How would I feel if it showed up RIGHT NOW?"

Did you feel overjoyed at that thought, or resistant?

If you felt a hesitation, that is part of you saying, "I'm not sure."

Listen to that voice. It's part of you, trying to get you to your ultimate happiness and comfort. It's looking out for you.

Honor it. Don't fight it.

Imagine creating a slightly lesser version of the dream and recheck how you might feel about that coming true in the present.

If you feel a yes, perhaps you can start with trying to manifest a slightly smaller step.

I know you can do it!

Remember that goat might seem slow, going step-by-step up the mountain, but he will still get to the top.

I hope that this book has helped you to understand your amazing ability to use frequencies and your power to create.

I believe in you!

Go forth and manifest all that you love my friends!

Afterwords

A bout my personal manifestation story…
I said I would tell you how it is that I am writing this book from a first class seat on my way home from China. It's been a year of traveling now, and here we are at the culmination of my book.

I told you I'd share my personal story about how my wish to ?y all over the world manifested.

I had spent most of my money for the last 20 years on 'mom' stuff, and traveling really hadn't been in my agenda or budget.

It wasn't until I did the simple exercise I advised you to try, that I discovered how much my spirit really wanted to travel and see things.

I'd been stuffing that part of me because I had too much responsibility and not enough money.

And even though, when you're an attractive woman, there's always some soul-less opportunity to cash in for money in Hollywood, it was something I would never consider, no matter how many offers lined up involving exotic travel with low-vibe companions.

Besides, what a cruddy manifestation that would be! Traveling with someone gross and no fun just because they could pay? Ugh!

My triangle would not have been happy with that manifestation option at all!

Shortly after this travel revelation and my doing my usual formula (which I just shared with you), my girlfriend Andrea came in to where I was working and offered to get me on the new *Survivor* show.

She had just returned from filming the show herself, and had been in some far-away land doing bizarre things, and in the end even won money.

I couldn't wait! This was my wish coming through! Did she actually say she could get me on the next episode?Wow! Yippee!!!!

I jumped up and down. I told everybody.

Joy! Joy! Oh my gosh! My wish is coming through!

I just wished to travel, and now I was going to be able to go someplace unique and fabulous! I even made a video about it, gushing about my excitement. Not to mention, once again, this was all manifesting for no cost to me, which I just think is so cool!

Once again, it proves that we don't have to rely on money, that the divine universe flows in and makes it happen, somehow, in a way we might have never imagined.

The next day, I wandered over to Facebook to go through my tons of friend requests that I hadn't even looked at. Yeah, I'm not so good at keeping up with the computer stuff. Anyway, at the top of all these friend requests was somebody I actually knew. It was an old junior high school classmate of mine, Dave. (Actually, he had been my first crush at seven years old, but I never told him). It was just before Christmas and I was going home to Buffalo.

Coincidentally, Dave had a business trip that canceled, and he was going to be home in Buffalo for the holidays as well. Both of our families and all of our high school friends still lived in Buffalo, so I was really excited to see everybody.

Dave called me up and we got together while we were both back home and we had a fabulous time.

Although neither one of us were looking for or ready for a relationship, somehow we just ended up — not being able to stay away from each other!

It doesn't sound so bad unless you don't live in the same city.

Still, we thought we could manage the distance thing because Dave is a pilot, and flying is what he does.

He flies big planes around the world (The Boeing 777) for a major American company.

California was just over yonder, to him! The only problem was that he was flying around the world so much, it was hard for us to get free time together to meet up.

It ended up that the best way for us to see each other was for me to go with him when he worked. Thus, I began to ?y with Dave on his trips so we could be together, and then, hello, guess what? I also got to travel to *London, Singapore, Dubai, and Hong Kong!*

Aside from the international travel, I have also visited every large city in America this year.

I ?y with him for free, the company puts him up at 5-star hotels for free, and when I'm extra lucky, I get bumped up to first class (and I've been extra lucky lately :-)).

Because we are a couple now, and the darling put me on his account, I can actually log in and **book myself a flight anywhere around the world, anytime I want, for free...**

So this is how my wish to travel the world came through in an awesomely beautiful and totally unexpected way!

How could I ever have begun to guess that two of my greatest dreams, to find love and to travel the world, would both show up together?!

I am so grateful and happy.

Now the world is the limit for us, and now also for you!

Remember, if I can do it you can do it.

Happy manifesting, my friends.

I love you!

******

Final thoughts

When you turn the page, Amazon will give you the opportunity to rate this book and share your thoughts through an automatic feed to your Facebook and Twitter accounts. If you believe your friends would get something valuable out of this book, I would be honored if you told them about your thoughts.

If you feel particularly strong about contributions this book made to your manifesting success, I'd be eternally grateful if you posted a review on Amazon.

Please visit me at my website, MorningMayan.com,

where I have the rest of my books and other tools that can help you manifest.

Contact me directly at MorningMayan.com for info on upcoming events, new books, or coaching. :)

If you would like to learn more about the basic science of frequencies, please get my book on Amazon —

Ultimate Power - The Universal Power of Love

I am excited to be releasing my complete book on frequencies, due out spring of 2015. This is my account of my near death experience and how I came to be contacted and speak with angels. It also includes both White Eagle's book on the science of frequencies, but also my 5 step manifestation process I developed to help you create anything you desire.

To Heaven And Back – The Complete Book On Frequencies

If you are interested in a pocket-sized version of the 5-step process, I also have an e-book abridged version called

Manifest in 5 Easy Steps

If you're interested in manifesting your perfect divine body and shape, please check out my diet book that released me from my own weight issues.

The California Diet

Please also follow me on YouTube as:

MorningMayan where I have several free videos on how to manifest and how to understand frequencies.

For complete info, go to <u>MorningMayan.com</u>

Please come over and join me socially on Facebook and Twitter as *MorningMayan*

Made in the USA
Middletown, DE
22 February 2016